Mahogany Musings

Poems For The People • Volume II

ROYAL ROOTS

TERESIA SIMMONS

Mahogany Musings Book Series, Poems for the People Volume II,
Royal Roots

Published in the United States, Aiseret Publishing.
Teresia.Simmons@gmail.com

First Edition
ISBN: 979-8-9859966-1-6

Dedication

To my son Randall, you are truly an example of passion and purpose. Thanks for making me a mother.

To my daughter Rabiah, whose spark gives me joy.

To my grandchildren Marqueze, DJ, Ja'Phia and London, who teach me what love really is.

Contents

Advice Unsolicited

You say stay and things will change
You say try again
Changes can be made

You say be patient
Things will get better

You say be more loving
You say no one is perfect
You say look at yourself

You say be grateful
You say everyone has problems

You say
You say
You say

I say let me alone
I say this is my life
I say these are my needs
I say these are my sorrows
I say this is my pain

Ultimately God alone knows my destiny

Meanwhile
I say I am doing my best
To do what is right for me

Thank you very much

Alphabet Soup

T stands for
Terrific personality
Togetherness
Toughness
Tenacity
Tenderness
Touching
Trying
Timing
Timid
Tremendous
Trepidation
Tranquil
Trembling
Tantalizing
Titillating
T equals me

This poem was one of my first, inspired by an
In-service training day for
Teachers in school.
They encouraged us to use creative writing and
Poetry to appreciate ourselves and then
To use the same technique to replicate
With the children.

A Mother's Love

A mother's love will transcend the ages.
A mother's love is unconditional.
Carried for nine months or nurtured for
Eighteen years and beyond.
A mother's love is without measure.
A mother's love is priceless.
The bond of love is found in the eyes.
In the heart.
In the mind.
Breast to mouth.
Soul to Soul.
Breath to breath.
A mother's love will outlast rebellion.
Famine.
Wars.
And the night.
A mother's love soothes the heart of a child.
And endures to the end, through eternity.
Her love travels in an endless
Circle of light and love.
When earthly bounds restrict and
Limit her body.
A mother's love lives on.
And on.
And on.

As I Write

As I write these words
When I put my pen to paper I wonder
Will you understand
What I am expressing and explaining?

Can you look within my heart and see my pain
My joy
My sorrow?

As I write these words
Should I write platitudes or
Simple topics without pain or strife?

Would that be easier for you?

This is my story
I am revealing my soul.

My stories
Soul revealing stories.

Is it me or a remnant of who I am?
Revealing my soul.

As I write...
Sometimes my beauty may be seen.
And sometimes the ugliness of life
May show its face.

This slice of the journey of my life
Show glimpses of moments of my life
That may be revealed,
And you may not like
What you see or hear.

But, it is my life, not yours.

So as I write,
I am allowing you for a few moments to
Glimpse into my life.

At The Beauty Shop

Early in the morning hours before daybreak
I prepare myself for the journey to my
Hairdresser at the beauty shop

Once there
I find joy
Friendly words spoken
Kindred spirits
Reinforcement of me
Amid the laughter
Are the shouts of my female compadres

Joy to the glory of being women
Laughter
Concerns
Kids
Men
Tales of lives lived
Wisdom shared

At the shop
Knowledge for life
Love and laughter
Early in the morning just before daybreak
I find myself
Rejuvenated

Refreshed
Permed and groomed
Soul and spirit filled with joy
Early in the morning
At the beauty shop
Where I find kindred spirits and friends

Beauty

Beauty is the wonder of your reflection
Within the mind's eye.

Beauty is the essence of you!

No one else can fulfill the uniqueness of you.

You are one in a million, beauty beyond
Compare.

Black Man

Power to the people.
Power to our people.
Black Power, Black powerful people.
Black Man.
He stands for hope, striving for commitment.
He stands for all those who can't
Speak for themselves.
He stands for truth no matter how painful.
He stands tall on the shoulders of those who are
Gone, yet present.
Martin, Medgar, Malcolm
Thurgood, Colin, Elijah
John.
Good Trouble.

Black Man
Symbols of hope, pride and joy.
Working hard, building, leading, guiding
Family and home.

Black man.
Standing firm.
Unafraid, unmoved, unbothered, uninterrupted.
Teaching and preaching
Against the wrongs.
Standing for the rights.

Transforming
Injustice, homelessness, poverty
Wars, hatred, envy, insecurity.

Keep on reaching
Fighting
Loving
Living
Fathering
Overcoming
Black Man
Keep on teaching so we remember how far
We've come.
Keep focusing on the future so we progress.
Freedom and equity.
Justice for all.
Justice for all our people.
Power to the people, our people
Black Man.

Brick House Queens

Nubian Queens
Regal
Statuesque
Heads above the crowds
Walking in stride
A confident glide
With floating movements and
Subtle swings of the hips
Exquisite
Black Queens
Crowned
Renowned
Beautiful
Dynamic
Classy
Fine
Brick House Queens

Brown Baby Boy

Sparkling baby boy with those great big eyes
In those small hands
My heart is yours.

One look
And I'm all aglow.

So unique and so sweet.
Another chance to share in the wonderment
Of a brand new life.

Sparkling brown baby boy with
Those great big eyes.
I love you and my heart is yours!

Clear Vision

Black man!
Can you see my ebony glow
Reflecting in the pools of your eyes?
I am you and you are me.

Images of royalty reign within this
Vision that you see.
My reality is you and your reality is me.

Strength to your strength
Joy to your joy
Sorrow to your sorrow
Passion to your passion
I am your counterpart
Your soul mate
Your reflection
Your reality.

Let us pool our resources and love
Creating a bond that will
Endure throughout eternity.

Black man, open your eyes and
See the reality of me, the reality of you
Of us
As one.

Daddy

Everybody knows "Big L"
He ain't that tall but he can surely
Take care of business.

Remember that time when we were sitting
On the front porch just talking
To the neighborhood boys and "Big L"
Came to the door and said,
"Didn't my wife tell you boys to go home?"
"Go Home!"
Shoot! Boys were running over themselves and
Over bushes trying to do
What "Big L" said.
I'm still laughing!!!
I've never seen a place clear out so fast!

"Big L"
Don't you remember when "Big L" took you to
The high school dance in the big red truck?
Everybody was just a looking and laughing.
"Be back here at 12 am sharp," said "Big L"
And I was.

"Big L"
Quiet, consistent and ever present.
"Big L" was there, and knew his purpose
He dared to parent!
The mold broke when he was made.
Memories come and go and they are always the
Same concerning
"Big L"
Solid and present.
Daddy "Big L"

Delay Or Decay

Delaying
Postponing
Procrastinating
Putting off
Neglecting

Missing
Deadlines
Opportunities
Possibilities

Why am I
Delaying
Obstructing
Doubting

My
Potential
Positivity
Greatness
Excellence

Delaying my
Destiny of
Magnificent
Capabilities

Did I?

Did I make my mark?
Did I grab a little corner of your heart?

Did my presence alert you to the
Genuine need to be loved and hugged?

Did I help you realize that love is
Tended carefully
Like a garden
Little by little each day?

Did I tell you or show you that
In some small way?

Did I make my mark?
Did I grab a little corner of your heart?

Do You!

Stop worrying about what others do,
Think or say!
Do you!
So it seems that they have more degrees,
More friends or more things!
Does it really matter?
The car! The man! The woman!
The! The! The!
Do you!
Examine your heart! Your goals! Your needs!
Your walk with the Lord!
Stop worrying about their needs, their desires!
Dare to be unique!
One of a kind!
Eccentric! Essential!
Be that magnificent creature!
Just do you!
Came into this world unique, one of a kind!
You broke the mold!
Why decrease?

Be that Queen!
That King!
Regal! Magnificent! Brilliant!
Have worries and concerns?
But!! But!! Be you!

Evolve into you!
Alone in birth! Triumphant in death!
Naysayers can't be you.
Jealous! Envious!
Player-Haters! Can't be you!
Can't clothe you. Can't feed you.
"Mouth all up on you!?!"
Be You! Not me! Not them!
Do you!
Be you!
Explore you! Empower you!
Do you my sistah!
Do you my brutha!
Do you!

Drums

The drums pulsate, pulsate filling my soul with
Primitive, primal desires
My feet take wings and move of their accord
The drums, drumming a passion
Respond to the raw rhythms
Pounding out their urgent primal beats
Somewhere inside
I am responding to the sounds of my soul
Images of dancers from long ago
Leap into my mind
My body vibrates to the ancient rhythms
Never taught
But my soul connects with those
Who have come before
The drums
The drums pulsate
Pulsate
Recalling the primal sounds and desires of my
Ancestors

Faith

The substance of things
Unseen and unknown
Faith to forget the past
And look to the future
Faith to try again
Faith to live
In the here and now
Knowing that
Through faith
Everything is possible

For My President

Barack Hussein Obama!
A Daniel, David, Solomon, Jeremiah
Rooted in Royalty.
I remain praying for your strength and wisdom
Regardless of your detractors, backbiters,
Player haters, gossipers, naysayers.
Keep the mission first.
Serve the people.

Remember the sacrifices of those
Unknown and unnamed.
Kings and martyrs who paved the way
With their blood, pain, tears,
Torment and anguish.
They are breathing into you their
Strength, hopes, and dreams.
Consider their sacrifices of
Broken bodies and spirits,
Spilled blood, indignities, slights, slanders.
Ruminate on the unreasonable demands.
Enslavement and
Persecution at the hands of their captors.
Paths blocked, joys deferred, split families
Murders and criminalization.

President Barack Obama!
I bequeath you soothing compassion
Healing balm for the pain.
Encouragement during moments of solitude.
Love when facing the unlovable.
Evoking those who paved the way for you.
Bloom and flourish through the
Rough, difficult, challenging and painful.

Through it all
The mission is to serve the people.
Remember the broken-hearted, lonely
Poor and the disenfranchised.
Those who cannot speak for themselves.
Remember the children
Remember the mission
Stand tall, through it all.

The mission continues.
Serve the people.

From Our Mommas

Dear chile
Dont fret, dont strain
We's come from great tribulations to reach
Where wes today
Ever day we rose at dawn
Prayin, workin, cleanin, bakin, rakin, slavin,
Dustin, plantin
Endless workin day by day
Never once losin faith wes gonna be free

Tha day come whar
We was no longa beholden ta no man
Free, free, yass we was
It was hard but de Lord said it
Wasnt gon be easy
Work and we work some mo
Lord, we schooled our chilren
Chile, they finished, degrees and all

We gots togetha changin thangs
Youse can sholl do the same
Tha goins may get a lil rough and it be so hard
Sometime but chile
Rise up, move on, there be too much
Work ta get done
Pray on it, plan on it, git ta goin

I don't wants no xcuses
Git ta gettin, bes on yo way
Wes not come this far ta give up
So chile
Keep pressin on, prayin on, reachin on
When youse tired, all worked up an wanna quit
Straighten yo back, stays on yo journey
God has plans for youse
Keep climbin honey
When youse reach your star
Remember thems who come before youse
Womens like Sojourner Truth, Harriet Tubman,
Sadie T.M. Alexander, Maggie Lena Walker,
Charity Earley, Rebecca Lee Crumpler
Yo Momma, my Momma an our
Mommas Momma
Thank thems
Shos them some hona
Youse have a legacy ta pass on ta other chilren
They needs youse today
Bes encouraged
Keep on a pressin
Make yo difference.

Happiness

Happiness is a shooting star blazing
Across the universe
A brilliant stream of glory
Stunning the eye of the beholder

Visionary pleasure that both
Frightens and draws one deeper
Into its glow
Brilliant, breathtaking and
Gone in fleeting seconds
Savored and remembered for its beauty.

Have You Ever Looked?

Have you ever looked at the
Faces of our children?
Have you looked at those sparkling brown eyes?
Have you planted seeds of
Knowledge and understanding?

Have you ever looked at the faces of our
Children
To see love shining in response to a kind word
A hug or a smile?

Have you ever looked at the faces of our
Children
When they are involved in a new adventure?
A new found discovery?
A new born puppy?

Have you ever looked into the faces of our
Children
And seen the mirror image of you?

Hey! Look at Me!

Hey, look at me!
I'm as surprised as I can be.
Is this really me?
Or is this a mirage that I see?
Could that discarded shell of a thing actually
Have been me?
There's no looking back.
There's no looking down!
A new horizon is in front of me!
Hey, look at me!
Can this creature actually be?
I'm exploring it
To become all
I can be.
I felt like a caterpillar but I've become
A
Flutterby.
Flutter, flutter,
Look at me!
Flutter, flutter, flutter!
Wow!
I am striking!
I am gorgeous!
I'm so beautiful!

Hey! Look at me!

Hope

The beginnings of a new day
New life
New way
Promises

New
Highlights
New hopes
For each day
Life and pathway
Promises

Lift
Hopes and dreams of
A new beginning
Promises of
New birth
New hope

I Am All That

You're trying to put me down.
I don't think so!
You see, I am THAT and I am all THAT!
I am God's child.

He didn't make me to cast down my eyes.
But lift them toward the sun.
My chest is raised high and proud.
I have nursed Kings and Queens at my bosom.
Put me down.
You can't!

You see, I am THAT and I am all THAT!
You can't put me down.
I am God's child.

Words said will stick to you and not TOUCH ME.
HATEFUL looks can't hurt me.
You see I am THAT, and I am all THAT!
I am God's child.

You say my lips are broad.
I call them luscious.
My nose is so wide.
I breathe in all of God's goodness.

My skin is brown.
It has been kissed by the sun.
My hips are expansive.
I bear beautiful sons and daughters.
Put me down you say?
I DON'T THINK SO!
I am God's child.

You can't put me down without my say so.
And I don't say so!

Don't you understand?
I am THAT! And I am ALL THAT!
I am God's child!

HE MADE ME THIS WAY ON PURPOSE
GOD MAKES NO MISTAKES!
He made me like THIS!
AND I AM ALL THAT!

I'm Still Here!

I'm still here though I was stolen
From my country
Forced to the coast
Shackled at the ankles
Collared by the neck
I survived and I'm still here!

I was thrown into the bowels of a ship
And forced to eat and live in my own filth
I survived and I'm still here
Beaten, raped, used, my body torn
Hung like fruit from a tree
But I'm still here!

Forbidden to learn how to read or write
Forbidden to go my own way
Forced to steal away
To pray and worship in the ancient ways
Still I survived and I'm still here!

Not allowed decent books, schools or even
Teachers
Still I learned, grew and flourished
And I'm still here!

I'm growing, learning and excelling
I'm teaching the young to survive and
Grow strong
Because I'm still here
I tell the stories
I'm still here!

And
I'm not going anywhere
So face me and smile
Because I'm still here!

I continue to survive
And I thrive!
Yes, I'm still here!

Images Of My People

Images burn within me of
Ancient rites
Ancient peoples
My people
Me.

Wisdom older than the sands of time
Colors of every hue
Innate knowledge
Distinguishable recognition
Shouts, cries, laughter, jealousy, hate, resilience
From the bowels of my being
Recognition
Our people, connected.

I see you, you see me.
I feel you, you feel me.

Acknowledging the experiences
The looks
The nod of the head
The bend of the neck
The sensitivity of the ear to
Recognized pain.

Disenchantment with the
Modern day system
Still
Blinded to the toils
Contributions
And sheer brilliance
Ancient people
Living people
My people
Me.

Unacknowledged
Power
Beauty
Uniqueness.

Ancient people
Living people
My people
Me
Invaluable.
Raw diamonds being polished
By the conditions of life
Burning
Refining
Molding
We are timeless masterpieces
Emanating throughout the ages.

In Between

Screaming into the world we come
Disconnected from the only womb of
Warmth and safety known
Growing older, bolder and more daring
Navigating and maneuvering our way
Through this world
Adventures, scrapes and some scars

Mending, healing
Some growth spurts
Rebellions
Leavings
Goodbyes and Hellos
Triumphs
Failures
Dormancy
Contentment
Resilience

Some unexpected experiences now and then.
Contemplations
Some regrets
Lives lived
Reflections
Breaking down and
Building up
Sadness and joys

Returning to the womb of the universe
Infinite wisdom
Joy
Comfort and light

Ascending into the eternity
Following the
Creator of Life
Into infinity
We go as
One

In My Blood

Never again will I believe the lies of
Negativity and shame attached to my people

In me flows the
Blood of Powerful Kings and
Strong Queens
In my blood flows the keys to
Secrets of the past
Discoveries of the universe

In me flows the blood of ancient mariners
Who sailed before Columbus and the Vikings
In me flows the blood of
Great warriors and world rulers
In me flows the
Blood of future generations
Of healers and teachers
Heads of State

In my blood lies greatness
In my blood flows the fate of this world and
Beyond

Never again will I believe their lies

Keep It Moving!

My essence disturbs you. Really?
You want me to shut up? Be calmer, act serene?
Not be so dramatic! Dull my senses?
Erase my intelligence?
Stay Silent?
Well... Keep it moving!

Does my light shine so bright that it is blinding?
Does it offend you? Bruise you? Frighten you?
Well! Enough already! Keep it moving!

No to the tomfoolery.
No to the subtle sighs and the wimpy cries.
I am enough. Been through enough!
Had enough! Always enough!
So keep it moving!

I am Black Girl Genius, Black Woman Magic!
I am Ancient Ancestor, Wisdom and
Mother Earth!
I am Brilliant! Empowered! Assured!
Daddy's girl. Momma's crown.
I am Glowing! Shimmering! Illuminating!
I am a light to all those who behold!

Are you insulted?
Trying to block me with your insecurity?
Are you angry?
Trying to suck the very life out of me
With your own insecurity!
Oh well!
Hasn't worked. Won't work!
I suggest you keep it moving!

Wanting me to shimmer less.
Dulling my essence?
Not a chance. Not a choice.
Never gonna be your reality.
So, take my advice and keep it moving!

Keep it moving!

Letter To My Daddy

Happy Father's Day, Daddy.

With all my love, I give you praise and thanks.
As scripture says,
"You have been faithful over a few things."

Having to figure it out for
Yourself most of the time.

Even when we, your children were trying your
Last nerves, you remained faithful and
Kept on doing your best.

I saw you
Working each day in a job that
Sucked your soul dry.
Never appreciated for all your excellent work.
You kept on anyhow.
Faithful until your retirement.
Didn't it take three men to replace you?

Past retirement, still getting up each morning
Doing your best...
Good or bad!
Still faithful in providing for your family.

Daddy, when you found the Lord
I admired and respected how
You continued to grow and
Remained faithful in service.
Still working, praying,
Being faithful to our Lord and King.

Thank you for being my Daddy.

"You have been faithful over a few things,
Therefore is laid up for you
A crown of righteousness."

I just know God shall receive you.
I can imagine Him saying

"Well done good and faithful servant, Sit down.
Take your rest. You can now rest in My arms."

With all my love,
Happy Father's Day
Today and every day!

Like A Bolt Out Of The Blue

On such a beautiful day
I was enjoying the sun basking on my face.
Hearing the sounds of golf balls and laughter
I could feel the sweat dripping off my brow.
The beauty of the course,
The green of the grass and
The blue of the sky was invigorating.

It was September 11, 2011.
Like a bolt out of the blue,
The word was heard, delivered by a
Ranger who shared the bad news.
"Have you heard the word?
The World Trade Center
Has been bombed in a terrorist attack."

Like a bolt out of the blue.
Televised images filled with
Clouds of destruction billowing.
We were not prepared for the avalanche of
Feelings, the onslaught of tears and anger.

Like a bolt out of the blue.
We were not prepared to see such
Heartache and despair
People plummeting like raindrops.

Falling from the sky.
Sirens screaming, complete chaos
Firefighters and police scrambling to
Aid those in need.
Families destroyed.
Lives lost.
Futures altered.

Like a bolt out of the blue, caught off guard.
We were not prepared. We were not aware.
We were not capable of comprehending this
Level of hatred, distrust and fear.
Passenger planes used as
Weapons of mass destruction
Like bolts out of the blue.

Spinning out of control.
Clamoring, grabbing, clutching
Trying to latch onto some sense of peace.
We were left uprooted, groundless.
Like bolts out of the blue.

Feeling powerless, blindsided by the
Vicissitudes of life, like a bolts out of the blue.
People of all faiths began to pray.

Living

Living takes
Courage, guts
Faith and perseverance.

Living requires
Reaching new potential
Risking, losing, gaining, and trying.

Living means
Exploring new frontiers.

Living is life.
Life is living.

Look At You!

Standing on the shoulders of your ancestors
Our people who withstood persecution
Survived the Middle Passage.
Treated worse than crazed animals
Raped, beaten, worked to death
Bodies not our own
Subjected to lynchings
And Jim Crow laws.

The prayers our ancestors prayed
Willing themselves to live.
Gathering strength to survive and endure.
Willing you their wisdom and power!

Gifted with the knowledge of Kings and Queens
Honoring their sacrifices.
Feel their presence surrounding and
Enveloping you with their
Essence, excellence and strength!
Look at you!

Your success has been paid by their blood!
The pride of our ancestors
Who know who you are!
Standing proudly and boldly beside you.
Succeeding, leading, nurturing!

The elders are watching.

Look at you!

Look at you, all aglow.

Basking in your intellect, class, ability,
Talents and accomplishments.

Look at you shimmering and shining
Profiling your excellence.
Their legacy.
Look at you.

Someone to Behold!
Lifting up the World!!
Yes, look at you!

Maturity

I thought that when I reached maturity...
Maturity? What is that?
Maturity? When is that?
Maturity! Is it ever a reality?

What is the magical age that we mature?
When do we finally have all the answers?
How do we know the path we're on for sure?

Maturity?
I thought when I was eighteen I was there.
At 21? Oh, I did not have a clue.
Still searching.
Still on my journey.

Maturity?
25? Well surprise, I'm still not there.
30's? Still rounding the curves of life.
40's? Interesting endeavors.

Maturity?
50's? Oooh, starting to look good...
Been a few places.
Seen some wear and tear in life.

Maturity?
60's? Still the journey of self-discovery.
Facing new challenges and different directions.
Outwardly, my face has changed, somewhat.
Reflecting on the erosion and etchings of life's
Passages impacting...
My face and physical being.

Maturity?
Inwardly...
Still the young woman, curious, daring and
Striving for maturity.
Still not there, but on the quest.
In the journey of becoming a beacon of wisdom.
Pointing the path to maturity.
Am I there yet?

Maturity?
Not yet!
Still seeking and striving.

Memories Float

So many memories float through my mind
Moments return
Some bittersweet
Some joyous
Some sensuous

Playful tugs of heart strings
Floating
Reflections of the past
Floating
Memories of times gone by
Floating and glowing

Metamorphosis

A cocoon
Dark, too tight, confining, small
A cocoon
Filled with one too fat and unappealing to be
Attractive
A cocoon
Safety inside
Warmth, needs met for a while
A cocoon
Strange stirrings within
Straining sounds and movements
Struggling to free the creature from its shell
Pop! Boom! Free!
A cocoon
A place of warmth by no freedom
Freedom
A new world unexplored
I have arrived freeing the shell of the past
To the freedom and unexplored frontiers of
Today
Free! Ever-evolving changes
A metamorphosis.

No Explanations!

I owe no explanations.

I function highly
In a world that may not accept me.

That's not my problem.
It is yours.

Get a life.

I am more than acceptable.
I am me.
I am worthy.
I love me.

No justifications.
No explanations needed.

No Regrets

To have loved deeply
Cherished richly
Lived immensely
I have no regrets
To have lived to this time and place
I have no regrets
Some setbacks
Some gains
Some pain
No Regrets
To have loved deeply
Cherished richly
Lived immensely
I have no regrets

Pain

This is a deep wrenching pain
My heart feels as though
It's been ripped out of my chest

I wanted more

You said
No

You said
You loved me and love was not enough

You told me
My pain will lessen and life will go on

You left me
Alone

I am in so much pain

Slowly
I am healing though still in pain

Pandemic

Covid 19 Novel Coronavirus
Plague
The Bible speaks of plagues past and future
God the Father was there, is here
And will be with us forever
Eternal guidance
Eternal love
Infinite
Unfathomable
Sovereign
Eternal light
Love
Leading
Calming
We are His glorious creations
Pandemic plagues are no match for our Father.

Pieces of Me

Scattered
Fragmented
Torn
Blown away just like the leaves in autumn
Falling dead, dry and drifting in the wind
Landing in places of desolation
Leading to my decay
Whirling
Twirling
Distractions
Unknown
Pieces of me blowing
Swirling into the unknown

Queens Are We

Really?

I am not the one to talk to if you cannot see the
Beauty and strength of the Black Woman!

Whatever continent we are on
Have been enslaved to
Or snatched from
Black women have had to fight for their lives
Their men and their children.

Don't go there with me.
Not when I saw my grandmothers,
My mother and myself
Fight physically, mentally and spiritually for the
Souls of our men and children.

We've stood firm in the face of racism,
Discrimination and hatred
Our bodies broken by those who've
Suppressed us
And by those who were supposed to love us.

Still we've supported and taken
Care of our folks, our families, and
Our people in spite of themselves.

In spite of ourselves
Broken, not of our own choosing.
Still striving to see the good
And loving in spite of the pain and sorrow.

We exhibit
The exquisite sacrificing pain of loving
Yet forgetting to love ourselves.

Enough! No more! Stop!
We have to save ourselves.
We must see our brilliance,
Our excellence!
Our glory!

Don't tell us we are not enough!
Been through enough!
We are enough!
Been enough!

Survived lies perpetrated by mouths that don't
Know our struggles or our pain.
Diminished by the status quo
By those not in the know.

Yet
A still soft voice stirs within.
We begin examining our beauty and strength
Reflecting amidst the pools of pain
Blood and rejection
Which cloaked the vision to see within.

The Queen has always been there, is here!
Strength willed to us!
Given from those who came before
A gift, a thirst that cannot be quenched.

My eyes are open now.
I can see my greatness displayed in
All of its glory.
I am present!
Present for me
Present to love freely
Present to love me
And all my magnificence
Not blinding myself, to my brilliance
To our brilliance
Queens are we.

Accepting who we are.
Our journeys of love and pain.
Queens are we.

Queens
Standing strong
Beautifully gowned
Straight crowns
In excellence
Queen are we.

That's the reality.

Reach Back

Echoes of the past
Reach back!
Memories of those who marched
Reach back!
Eyes wide open to the deceits of yesteryear
Reach back!
Open faces eager to learn
Reach Back!
Feed my children things they need to prosper
Reach Back!
You are only as big as those
You stoop to help
Reach Back!
We need you
We are waiting
Reach Back!
Therein lies our strength
Reach Back!
Echoes of the past leaning toward
Visions of the future
Reach Back!

Richness

Don't you want to feel my wide lips?
My supple, ample hips?
My richness?
My lushness?
Suckle my breasts
And rest in my
Strong, sturdy arms.
I am your Queen
Your Nefertiti.
I am the mirror reflection of you
Smoky, inviting and
Cool like the night.
I'll be your Queen
To share your Throne
And abide by your side.
Come my King.
Build an Empire of Love.
Combining the dark pool
Of our blood and Love
Feel my lips!
My supple hips!
My richness!
My lushness!
My love!

Say My Name!

From the bowels of the earth
My blood will speak
God don't like ugly!
He does not forget!
The sins of the fathers will be visited on the
Children and
Their children's children.

No Ma'am!

You may not call me by my first name.
No, you may not touch my hair or my body
Without my permission.
I have my Boundaries!!!
Say my Name!

No you may not!
I speak for those who could not or cannot speak
Because their voices were silenced.
Respect delayed.
Finally given and granted
Earned dignity.
Queens who now know their worth

Confident in their own
Skin!
Say my name!

Shout it out loud!
Declare it for all!!
And the universe will hear it and rejoice!!
SAY MY NAME!!

Still I Teach

I am a teacher and I am not ashamed.
I touch the future.
I teach the children who may be
Left out, neglected and abused
Still I teach.

Each day I reach into my soul
And share with a mind that is fertile and
Ready for knowledge
Some must be coerced, coaxed and
Charmed to learn.
Still I teach.

I wear the countless hats of
Mother, nurse, babysitter, scholar, negotiator
Counselor and friend.
I am a mentor, a soother, a hugger, a
Fixer-upper, a bandage carrier, and an advisor.
Still I teach.

I care when an idea is finally
Mastered by a child.
I care when the physical ability changes and
New skills are mastered.
I care when I see the light in a child's eyes and
New confidence soars.
Still I teach.

I teach for myself because I care.
I teach for children because I care.
I care and I will continue to care.
I touch the future
And I'm proud to be there.
Still I teach!

Strength

Strength is sometimes a curse,
Not always a blessing.
Why must I be the strong one?

When do I get a chance to rest and
Have moments of weakness
And a shoulder to lean on?

I need
Encouragement
Hugs
Rest
And reassurances that
Everything will be alright.

I am so tired of being the one to be strong.
I need a person like me who will be
Tough, tender and true.

Strength can seem to be a curse
Though it is a blessing.

It depends from which angle
You are viewing.

Strides

My legs are a little wobbly
I am trying out my new supports

Walking gingerly
Taking small steps
Crashing down and getting back up again

I keep trying
Wobbling
Getting stronger each day
Strengthening
Priming
Shaking

But standing alone
And on my own

Talks Too Much!

They say
You talk too much!

I ask
Why is what I have to say
So real that you don't choose to hear?

Well back off!

I will continue to talk too much!
Express myself!
Define myself!
Support myself!
And
Defend myself!

I must be all that I can be.
I am funny and loud.
I laugh with total abandonment.
I love life and people.
I am exploring new avenues.

Stretching my
Boundaries and my Horizons.
Yes!
I talk too much at times.
And I love too much
Sometimes.

I embrace all of me!
And all of my life!

Yes!

I talk too much.
And I am proud of myself!

I love me.
I am living my life to the max!

Tell The Story

How do I tell you I'm having trouble?
How do I tell you in words?
The feelings I've had as a mother
When I could not protect my child
Against the words and cloaked daggers that
Tear the flesh and wound the
Minds and spirits of my innocent children?

Eyes so full of wonder and joy
Looking up to you
Asking for you
Pleading for you to take this pain away.
My child! My life!
Momma cannot protect you from this pain.
I can make you look into the eyes
Of this evil and recognize this demon!
This rotten apple that poisons the
Innocence of childhood.
My children, you are so precious!
Stand tall and proud as a child of the sun.
God blessed you as the first
People of this world.
You are a promise.
You are our future.

Never forget the elders who survived the
Middle Passage of slavery.
You have been willed their wisdom
Their courage and pride.
Stand tall in the sun.
Continue to tell the story.
You have a right to all the fruits in the garden.
Look upon this situation and
Compare it to the snake
That beguiled the woman causing her to sin.
See this creature for what it really is!
Hatred! Racism! Prejudice!
Stand shoulder to shoulder with your ancestors.
The shield and armor is in your hands.
Stand tall!
You are worthy of greatness.
Never let adversity,
Heartaches, ignorance or racism
Allow you to forget or doubt
Your greatness!
Live the dreams of those who have come before.

Momma can't always protect you
But I can surely mentor you and
Help direct your paths
Toward positivity and creative mobility.
Continue to pray on.

Walk on, fight on.
Lead the way for those who will be coming.
Direct your eyes forward and
Upward to the future.
But you must remember to tell the story.
Tell the story.

The Love Of A Woman

If a man could just understand a woman's
Need to feel like she is his Queen.

That
She is loved
Deserved and
Needed
Then anything is possible.

When a woman feels she is the sexiest
Thing on earth and
She can make her man's heart quiver
Then anything is possible.

If a man really looked into the heart of this
Woman
He would find
Love
Caring
Commitment
Joy
And a friend.

If a man can
Understand that he only has to look
For joy
To the woman standing by his side
Then anything is possible.

If a man can
Understand
He would, could and can have all the
Joy his heart can hold.
Then anything is possible.

They Came Singing Songs

When I think about my youth
I remember the women my
Momma invited over
They would eat and laugh and sing.

Momma was known for her cooking and her
Wonderful cakes and pies.

I would sit upstairs by the heat pipe and
Listen and laugh at their jokes and
The things they said.

Momma would've had a fit if she had known
I wasn't supposed to be listening to
Grown folks conversations.
The old folks would say
"Little pitchers have big ears."
"Girl, that child must be smelling herself"
She must think she is "grown or something."

I just couldn't help it.
I was drawn to their sights, sounds and smells.
Oh, and could they sing!
I would sing along, yet not too loud
To keep my secret.

I listened to their
Grown folks conversations
The colors, smells and sounds of those women
Who looked so much like me.

Voices lifted in songs of Zion
Shouted and praised the Lord.
Ms. Yvonne stomped a hole in the floor
Pounding out the beat of the song.

Singing, shouting, praising
Treasured memories.
I listened, and I listened.
In heaven, I imagine they are still
Singing, shouting, praising.
Singing up on high
Shouting
Hallelujah! Amen!

I made it over!
The messages and melodies left behind are
Engraved in my heart and my mind.
The women who came together singing praises,
Oh, how they sang and
Praised the Lord in spirit and song.

To My Black Men

Thank you for
Your persistence and
Your courage to take a stand in the
Raging winds of time when to do so
Could mean sudden death.

Thank you for your gnarled hands and limbs
Which withstood the beatings, the hoses and
The dogs of yesteryear.

Thank you men of color who risked death to
Escape enslavement.

Thank you bards of old who let your
Voices ring out, creating songs of joy, sadness,
Protest and commitment.

Thank you men of every hue from the
Blackest Black to the lightest hues,
For loving me, for seeing the beauty of my
Ample bosom and supple thighs.

Thank you for giving me your seed to
Produce strong, healthy children.

Thank you for reaching out to enclose
Caress and enfold me within your arms.

Thank you for sharing your pain
And your joy.

Thank you men of color for being there,
For striving to make this a better place
For your children and for me.
Though cast down and sometimes cast aside,
You have withstood the test of time.
Thank you for striving on anyhow.

Thank you for your prayers on
Bended knee to a Savior who remembered me.

Thank you for gentle hands that have
Shaped the minds and
Bodies of the young.

Thank you men of color in the
Fight for human dignity
Throughout the world.

Our seed needs and thanks you for your
Legacies.

Tread Mill

Learning to adjust to life
Is like
Living on a treadmill
One can choose to run themselves
To death in their frantic drive for excellence
Or
One can take the time to
Step-off
Rest and
Taste the beauty along the way

Contemplate and
Appreciate the
Beauty of just being alive

Two Became One

We two are still one
Separate entities with
Different issues
Different outlooks

We two are still one
Each one with
Uniqueness
Each one with gifts
We two must bridge the gap and merge our
Joys
Sorrows
Likes
Dislikes
Ways

We two are still one
Separate yet joined

We two who are one must merge
Share and evolve into intimacy
Not just physical
Not just external but internal too

We two who are one must celebrate
The love and mystery of two who become one
Each day a journey of oneness
Our final solace will be as one

We have shared the time
And chance of two who became one

Web

Fragile cobweb-like
Network of information
One lie breaks the thread
Too much tension and too much deceit
The thread shatters
Broken in twain
Trust in time and it
It builds a unit of connecting threads
Weaving and evolving
Into a unique of web
Of truth and love

Wedding Wishes

In this special moment you are
Dedicating your love and
Commitment to each other and
To your marriage.
You must each day find ways of sharing
Growing, defining, redefining
Negotiating, crying, forgiving, praying
Yielding, submitting
Respecting, seeking boundaries and
Setting boundaries.

On this journey of connecting and of caring.
On this journey of putting each
Other's needs first.
It's about pride and love for each other.

Basking in the joy of each other's
Accomplishments and talents.
It's about the wonder of you, together.
It's about God and His purpose
For your marriage.
His purpose for you both.

Paraphrasing Jesus,
"Where two or three are gathered in my name
There I am also."
Let this marriage be founded and grounded in
The principles of God's love and His love for us.

In this special moment, please remember that
It's not about me, but it's about we.
It's about a committed journey based on
God's love for the church.

Hold your love close and your hurts far away.
Keep the flame of love alive through your faith
Courage, commitment, communication and
Desire for a we, not a me, relationship.

When it's all said and done, and
In the years to come
It is our hope, that the two of you
Will still continue to look at
Each other in love.
And with love say
"Grow old with me, the best is yet to be."

God bless your marriage from this moment on
As you move from me to we, with love.
Wedding wishes with love.

What Do I Tell My Children?

How do I tell them?
How do I tell them that the world
May not treasure their Blackness?
How do I tell them that they will feel the
Pain of exclusion and elimination?
How do I tell them that the world will judge
Them on their color first
Then their character?
How do I tell them that the hurt will continue
Unless hearts, lives and
Thought patterns are changed?
How do I tell them?
I tell them the truth!

I tell them to persevere anyhow.
To face the world and
Dream their dreams
Anyhow.

I tell them their history and herstory.
Their royal roots, their divine connection.
I tell them of the elders who lived through the
Pain and survived to fight on.
I tell them of my struggles and of those who
Have gone before me.

I tell them!
I tell them the secrets of surviving the journey.
Their inborn power and fortitude.
I tell them to keep the fires of hope burning
Inside the core of their souls.
I keep telling them!

I tell them lovingly, with patience,
Courage, and strength.
I tell them I love them and will continue to
Love them throughout the ages.
I tell them as the ancient griots told the
Tales so the history of our
People will not be lost.

Tell the children
As they become the keepers and
Rulers of this world.

Will It Happen?

Have you ever thought...
Will each postponement mean the end of
Dreams?
A gift given not to come to pass?
Life is getting in the way.
I think not.

Is it meant to be?
Can anyone take it away from me?
I think not.

Patience is in your heart.
Has always been from the start.
Gifts have been given, free to be claimed.
Blessings designated in your name.

Stay true to your dreams.
Hold to your goals.
Believe in yourself.

Delays, pot holes, side roads and setbacks
Devised to make you strong.
And yes, the road's been long.
Your gifts are your gifts.
Get ready, prepare to launch!
It's time to fly.

Why Didn't You Tell Me?

Why didn't I know?
You didn't tell me.

Why didn't you tell me that I am a Queen?
I am intelligent.
Worthy of honor.
Deserving of care and respect.

Did you not think I was worth being
Valued?

If you don't tell or show me
How will I know?

When I look around
What will I see if I look on social media?
Do I see positive images of women
Who look like me?
Or do I see booty shaking, breast bearing
Ladies of the night?
Do I see educated women?
Scientists, entrepreneurs, politicians
Wise mothers?
Teachers?
Women who have ruled and
Changed the world?

Did you read me books of their excellence?
Did you take me to the museums
Showcasing the
Arts and our history?

I am just a little girl.
Did you hug me, kiss and cherish me?
Did you tell me that I am beautiful
Smart and outstanding?

If not?
How was I supposed to know
I am a Queen
To be valued and treasured?

Wisdom

The older I get
The smarter my mother becomes.
"Time heals all wounds,"
"Keep your peace,"
"Mind your manners,"
And
"Respect your elders,"
She would say.

When I was young
I laughed at her because I didn't comprehend.
Now I understand.
I don't laugh anymore, I listen.

The older I get
The smarter my mother becomes.
Now I stop and I listen.
I really listen.

Young Warrior

How many more must die
Fighting violence against violence
Young Warriors?

How many more must die in your endless
Pursuit of money and material gain
Young Warriors?

How many more of our precious
Black men must die before you realize that
Manhood is not a measure of might against
Might but respect vs. respect
Young Warriors?

Is there another way for you to get your propers
Without this display of self-hate
Young Warriors?

Please!
We have already lost generations to
Drugs, prisons and death.

Find a way to treat each other with
Respect and love not self-hatred.
We need you if we are to survive
Young Warriors!

Please!
We need your strength and power to lead.
Stop the Killings!

Please!
You are our future and
We cannot afford to lose any more!
Stop the killings, please!

We love you
Young Warriors!

Acknowledgements

I give all honor and glory to my precious Lord for His gift of Jesus and the gifts that He has given to me. I thank Him for His love, guidance and protection.

To Jo Lena Johnson of the Absolute Good Enterprises Publishing Company for seeing the value of my poetry and your earnest and wholehearted support of my writing. Thank you. And the fact that you are my Soror is just so awesome.

To my parents, Lela and Leonard Hall who've always had faith in me. Thanks for your prayers, guidance, spiritual training, sacrifices and your absolute love for me, and for supporting my educational goals and my children. Also, for teaching me to value and love myself, our culture, and our family.

I am grateful for my church families throughout my life: Mt. Zion Missionary Baptist Church in Springfield, Ohio - the late Pastor Rev. W.E. Richardson, Sr., Shiloh Baptist Church in Dayton, Ohio - the late Pastor H. L. Parker. Mt. Zion Baptist Church in East St. Louis, Illinois- the late Pastor John H Rouse. My present church,

Friendly Temple Missionary Baptist Church in St. Louis, Missouri - Bishop Michael F. Jones, Sr. Each of these church families and pastors nurtured my life through their leadership, guidance and biblical teachings.

I am thankful for being a member of Delta Sigma Theta Sorority, Inc., and to my line sisters of the Dayton Alumnae Chapter, La Grande Premiere Fall 1988, who have supported and encouraged me every step of the way. Special love to Beverly Moody and Rachel Johnston. To the St. Louis Alumnae Chapter, special thanks to the Sorors on the June Luncheon Committee who encouraged me to write a poem dedicated to our sisterhood.

To the Redman Writers Guild under the leadership of Dr. Eugene Redmond who welcomed me at all their events with open arms. I especially thank Darlene Roy, also a Delta Soror, who continued to reach out and encourage me. I thank Joyce McKinney for the introduction.

To my St. Louis Sister Friends who have never stopped believing in me: Jeane, Dorothy, Kimberly, Gloria, Georgia, Kwamina, Ruth, NJ, and Mary.

Thanks to Deborah Bennett Peterson who gave me an opportunity to present my poetry at the African Heritage Gala in 1993, at the Dayton

Art Institute for the DCDC Associates. What a memorable experience! This gave me the desire and courage to publish my poetry. Thanks for your unfailing love and support.

To the Ferguson Writers Group with whom I have been a member for well over a decade, our writing retreats and your creative inspiration have been a blessing. And, to Mrs. Carolyn Herkstroeter whose love and encouragement never wavered in wanting to see me as a published poet. Thank you for the opportunity to give a poetry reading to your chapter of the Association of American University Women.

To my Heavenly Angels whose support kept me writing and gave me inspiration because of your love: MaryAnne Mehaffie, Nancy Cox, Craig Wallace, Vinson Taylor and Deanna Mills. Each of you are missed and hold a piece of my heart.

To my lifelong friend Marva Boswell and my cousin Carol Thompson. There's so much to be said for over 60 years! Thanks for being you.

To my 50 year friends, Elaine Stringer and Carolyn Jackson. You are some of the most loving and caring people on this earth. Thank you.

To Marilyn Williams, my friend and fellow member of the Evermoor's. That poetry convention in Washington D.C. was an invaluable experience. Being with you where we were surrounded by published poets, jump started our forty plus year bond as teachers and writers. Thank you!

To Melba, Wyomina, Flora June, Lisa, Lita and Denise, whose love and support are never ending.

To my spiritual "ride or die" sisters whose prayers of love and support have enabled me to continue healing throughout these many years of rough spots. Marva, Yvonnejannai, Lena, Minnie, Crystal, Jacquelyn, Bernice, Carolyn and Pam. And Stephanie, your prayers along with keeping me close when I needed a friend who understood what losing a spouse entailed were lifesaving.

To my siblings Anthony, Christopher and Karen, sister-cousins Monica, Carol and Andrea, thanks for the love we've shared. To my late sister Gloria and Aunt Elverta, I miss you and love you.

To my late husband Joe Simmons who would have been bursting with pride and love to see me performing and signing my books, thank you, my forever and a day love for your support.

About the Author

Author Teresia Simmons grew up in Springfield, Ohio. She is the second child of Lela and Leonard Hall, the second of five children and the first-born daughter. Her parents were married for sixty-four years before her father passed away in 2011. Shortly after, her family mourned the loss of her younger sister, Gloria.

She earned a B.S. in Education from Eastern Kentucky University and a M.S. in Education with special emphasis in Physical education and Dance from the University of Dayton. She became the first African American employee in the Englewood, Ohio, Northmont City Schools, served as a Physical Education teacher.

She married her first husband, Roy Harper in 1971 and from this union, they adopted two children, Randall and Rabiah. The marriage dissolved in after 12 years. She married Joe Simmons in 2000.

She also taught as an adjunct professor at the University of Dayton and Sinclair Community College. She finished her career at Clayton, retiring after thirty years. After marriage, she settled in St. Louis, Missouri, where she became a certified teacher for the Normandy, Jennings and Ferguson Florissant School Systems.

In 2010, Teresia Simmons began working with a small fitness studio, doing individual coaching and teaching in fitness and weight management until her husband Joe was diagnosed with Dementia and needed full time care. He succumbed to the disease in 2019. During that journey, she found great support while volunteering with the Greater Saint Louis Chapter of the Alzheimer's Association, and is now a trained Volunteer Educator. She has also been actively involved with the Friendly Temple (Church) Alzheimer's Support Group, the only African American focused support group in the area.

At present, she is completely retired and loving it. Teresia is an Advisory Board Member and a 17 year member of the St. Louis Symphony Orchestra InUnison Chorus. She also devotes her time volunteering and serving as a member of Friendly Temple Missionary Baptist Church Health Committee, singing in the choir, and helping with the Repast Committee. She is also a member of the Delta Sigma Theta Sorority, Inc., Saint Louis Alumnae Chapter.

Author Teresia Simmons travels and continues to hone her craft by attending writing and poetry workshops, as she finds great joy in creating works of art based on her vast life experiences, including the joy, pain and commitment of love, sickness and health.